CAPRICORN

~SUN SIGN SERIES~

T0307067

CAPRICORN

SUN SIGN SERIES

JOANNA MARTINE WOOLFOLK

TAYLOR TRADE PUBLISHING

LANHAM • NEW YORK • BOULDER • TORONTO • PLYMOUTH, UK

Published by Taylor Trade Publishing
An imprint of The Rowman & Littlefield Publishing Group, Inc.
4501 Forbes Boulevard, Suite 200, Lanham, Maryland 20706
www.rlpgtrade.com

Estover Road, Plymouth PL6 7PY, United Kingdom

Distributed by National Book Network

British Library Cataloguing in Publication Information Available

Library of Congress Cataloging-in-Publication Data

Woolfolk, Joanna Martine.
  Capricorn / Joanna Martine Woolfolk.
    p. cm.—(Sun sign series)
  ISBN 978-1-58979-562-4 (pbk. : alk. paper)—ISBN 978-1-58979-537-2 (electronic)
  1. Capricorn (Astrology) I. Title.
 BF1727.65.W66 2011
 133.5'275—dc23   2011018434

∞™ The paper used in this publication meets the minimum requirements of American
National Standard for Information Sciences—Permanence of Paper for Printed Library
Materials, ANSI/NISO Z39.48-1992.

I dedicate this book to the memory of
William Woolfolk
whose wisdom continues to guide me,

and to
James Sgandurra
who made everything bloom again.

CONTENTS

ABOUT THE AUTHOR

Astrologer Joanna Martine Woolfolk has had a long career as an author, columnist, lecturer, and counselor. She has written the monthly horoscope for numerous magazines in the United States, Europe, and Latin America—among them *Marie Claire*, *Harper's Bazaar*, *Redbook*, *Self*, *YM*, *House Beautiful*, and *StarScroll International*. In addition to the best-selling *The Only Astrology Book You'll Ever Need*, Joanna is the author of *Sexual Astrology*, which has sold over a million copies worldwide, and *Astrology Source*, an interactive CD-ROM.

Joanna is a popular television and radio personality who has been interviewed by Barbara Walters, Regis Philbin, and Sally Jessy Raphael. She has appeared in a regular astrology segment on *New York Today* on NBC-TV and on *The Fairfield Exchange* on

CT Cable Channel 12, and she appears frequently on television and radio shows around the country. You can visit her website at www.joannamartinewoolfolk.com.

ACKNOWLEDGMENTS

Many people contribute to the creation of a book, some with ideas and editorial suggestions, and some unknowingly through their caring and love.

Among those who must know how much they helped is Jed Lyons, the elegant, erudite president of my publishers, the Rowman & Littlefield Publishing Group. Jed gave me the idea for this Sun Sign series, and I am grateful for his faith and encouragement.

Enormous gratitude also to Michael K. Dorr, my literary agent and dear friend, who has believed in me since we first met and continues to be my champion. I thank Michael for his sharp editor's eye and imbuing me with confidence.

Two people who don't know how much they give are my beloved sister and brother, Patricia G. Reynhout and Dr. John T. Galdamez. They sustain me with their unfailing devotion and support.

We are born at a given moment, in a given place, and like vintage years of wine, we have the qualities of the year and of the season in which we are born.

CARL GUSTAV JUNG

INTRODUCTION

When my publishers suggested I write a book devoted solely to Capricorn, I was thrilled. I've long wanted to concentrate exclusively on your wonderful sign. You are very special in the zodiac. Astrology teaches that Capricorn is the sign of extraordinary achievement and enduring devotion. Your sign represents determination and discipline, lofty ambition, and an enterprising nature. You have integrity, patience, superior intelligence, and an intensely loving heart. Especially, you're known for your leadership abilities—you are devoted to excellence. Karmic teachers say you were specially picked to be Capricorn because in a previous life you received high honors and were a builder of something enduring. But whether or not one believes in past lives, in *this* life you are Capricorn, the remarkable sign of wisdom, constancy, and the power to accomplish.

These days it has become fashionable to be a bit dismissive of Sun signs (the sign that the Sun was in at the time of your birth). Some people sniff that "everyone knows about Sun signs." They say the descriptions are too cookie-cutter, too much a cardboard figure, too inclusive (how can every Capricorn be the same?).

Of course every Capricorn is not the same! And many of these differences not only are genetic and environmental, but are differences in your *charts*. Another Capricorn would not necessarily have your Moon sign, or Venus sign, or Ascendant. However, these are factors to consider later—after you have studied your Sun sign. (In *The Only Astrology Book You'll Ever Need*, I cover in depth differences in charts: different Planets, Houses, Ascendants, etc.)

First and foremost, you are a Capricorn. Capricorn is the sign the Sun was traveling through at the time of your birth.* The Sun is our most powerful planet. (In astrological terms, the Sun is referred to as a planet even though technically it is a "luminary.") It gives us life, warmth, energy, food. It is the force that sustains us on Earth. The Sun is also the most important and pervasive influence in your horoscope and in many ways determines how others see you. Your Sun sign governs your individuality, your distinctive style, and your drive to fulfill your goals.

Your sign of Capricorn symbolizes the role you are given to play in this life. It's as if at the moment of your birth you were pushed onstage into a drama called *This Is My Life*. In this drama, you are the starring actor—and Capricorn is the character you play. What aspects of this character are you going to project? The Capricorn diligence, creative drive, and strength of character? Its refinement and love of knowledge? Or its avariciousness, insensitivity, emotional coldness, and materialism? Your sign of Capricorn describes your journey through this life, for it is your task to evolve into a perfect Capricorn.

For each of us, the most interesting, most gripping subject is *self*. The longer I am an astrologer—which at this point is half my lifetime—the more I realize that what we all want to know about

*From our viewpoint here on Earth, the Sun travels around the Earth once each year. Within the space of that year, the Sun moves through all twelve signs of the zodiac, spending approximately one month in each sign.

is ourselves. "Who am I?" you ask. You want to know what makes you tick, why you have such intense feelings, and whether others are also insecure. People ask me questions like, "What kind of man should I look for?" "Why am I discontented with my job?" or "The man I'm dating is an Aries; will we be happy together?" They ask me if they'll ever find true love and when they will get out of a period of sadness or fear or the heavy burden of problems. They ask about their path in life and how they can find more fulfillment.

So I continue to see that the reason astrology exists is to answer questions about you. Basically, it's all about *you*. Astrology has been described as a stairway leading into your deeper self. It holds out the promise that you do not have to pass through life reacting blindly to experience, that you can within limits direct your own destiny and in the process reach a truer self-understanding.

Astrologically, the place to begin the study of yourself is your Sun sign. In this book, you'll read about your many positive qualities as well as your Capricorn issues and negative inclinations. You'll find insights into your power and potentials, advice about love and sex, career guidance, health and diet tips, and information about myriads of objects, places, concepts, and things to which Capricorn is attached. You'll also find topics not usually included in other astrology books—such as how Capricorn fits in with Chinese astrology and with numerology.

Come with me on this exploration of the "infinite variety" (in Shakespeare's phrase) of being a Capricorn.

Joanna Martine Woolfolk
Stamford, Connecticut
June 2011

CAPRICORN

DECEMBER 22–JANUARY 19

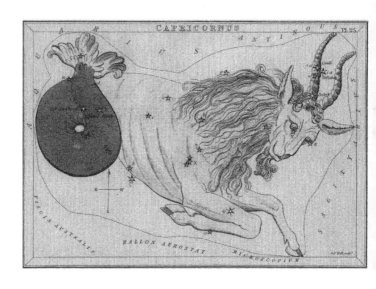

PART ONE

ALL ABOUT YOU

ILLUMINATING QUOTATIONS

"Ambition is a dream with a V-8 engine."

—Elvis Presley, rock and roll icon, a Capricorn

"My goal is simple. It is a complete understanding of the universe, why it is as it is, and why it exists at all."

—Stephen Hawking, physicist and cosmologist, a Capricorn

"I want to be what I've always wanted to be—dominant."

—Tiger Woods, professional golfer, a Capricorn

"Some think the way to be big is to shout and stomp and raise hell, and then nothing ever happens. I'm not like that. I never shoot blanks."

—Richard M. Nixon, thirty-seventh president of the United States, a Capricorn

"I pretended to be somebody I wanted to be until finally I became that person. Or he became me."

—Cary Grant, actor, a Capricorn

"Attitude is everything."

—Diane von Furstenberg, fashion designer, a Capricorn

YOUR CAPRICORN PERSONALITY

....

YOUR MOST LIKEABLE TRAIT: Steadiness

....

The bright side of Capricorn: Patient, committed, responsible,
    determined, disciplined
The dark side of Capricorn: Rigid, overly exacting, pessimistic,
    opinionated, materialistic

*You're born with an appetite for achievement and triumphing over
the odds. You take pride in what you do—you have ideals and
expectations, and are never satisfied with being mediocre. You're
persistent and courageous, possessing dignity and refinement. Capricorn represents the top of the zodiac, its zenith, and your drive is
to reach the heights. Your instinct is to rule, and when you use this
appropriately, you don't lord it over others but have full control
over your own work, career, and creativity. An endearing trait is
your dry sense of humor, as well as your loyalty and capacity for
friendship. Still, in great contrast to your self-assured manner, your
inner confidence tends to be shaky, which results in dictatorial and
autocratic behavior. Often beset by Saturnian heaviness, you need
to consciously lighten your outlook and attitude.*

Capricorns are ambitious, and the lives of those born under this sign are marked by a purposeful pursuit of their destiny. Your motivating force is desire for success, money, status, position, authority, and (though you may not realize it) love.

Capricorn is both an Earth sign and a Cardinal sign, and the combination of practicality (Earth) and initiative (Cardinal) produces a personality geared toward leadership and power. In the zodiac, Capricorn is linked to the Midheaven—the point at the top of the horoscope that represents high achievement. You're a born climber who's not content to poke along down in the valleys. As long as there is a top to get to from the bottom, you will persevere in your upward striving. Your symbol is the Goat, and everyone knows how goats bound up impassable terrain, finding footholds where no one thought they existed. You always carry with you the knowledge that there are tasks to be fulfilled, and if you can't move mountains, then at least, like the Goat, you can scale the heights.

Your ruler, Saturn, is the planet of limitations, which includes the limitation of time. (To the ancients, Saturn was the symbol for Father Time.) You have a heightened sense of the value of time, which helps to make you a superb organizer and planner. Unlike those who don't look beyond next month, you will carefully examine your goal, separate it into all its necessary steps, and plot out a long-term timetable that often involves years. In the sign of Capricorn, the quality of patience reaches new heights. One of the hallmarks of your sign is that you learn to wait for the things you want. You are willing to give up today's temptation for tomorrow's reward.

An aura of melancholy and sternness often surrounds you. Saturn has been called the Celestial Taskmaster, for it symbolizes responsibility, discipline, and restriction. Saturn teaches lessons in endurance—and with this planet as your ruler, you're ambitious, practical, and above all, determined. As a child of Saturn, you need something to improve and to perfect. You could have been the prototype for Lewis Carroll's droll jingle about industriousness: "How doth the little crocodile improve its shining tail?"

You are not interested in vague theory; you want to put any knowledge to use. Your active mind quickly grasps ideas, and you have an admirable ability to concentrate. You are precise and orderly, have excellent judgment, and generally don't trust others to look after details. You want to make sure all contingencies are covered—it's your way of being in control. Without seeming to be in a hurry, you accomplish more than the frantic, harried people. This is due to your singleness of purpose and to the fact that you have the stamina of a marathon runner. When you give your word, you stick to it. And when you undertake a task, you complete it to the best of your ability.

Because of your diligence, people sometimes fail to give you credit for creativity. Yet you are highly creative—your skill is to link this to your talent for organization. You use your time and talents to best advantage; you throw yourself into a project, learn all you can, and then begin to create on your own. You turn dreams into action. Your flair for the dramatic shows up as personal style and elegance, and in your superb taste. You're especially drawn to the artistic arena and the performing arts.

You think of yourself as a real person in a real world that allows little time for idle pleasure seeking. You search for permanence and channel your energies into accomplishment. Even when you were little, you took responsibility seriously. In certain ways, Saturn is an austere and strict parent that lives inside each Capricorn, enforcing rigid rules. Essentially, you feel you can depend only on yourself. The child within you feels unworthy—and your lifelong lesson is to shed this feeling and learn to love *yourself*. You do not need to be your own parent who disciplines and keeps you toeing the line. You yourself must allow the spontaneous part of you to play and run.

Your remoteness of spirit is often misunderstood by others; it has been described as cold passion. But you are not cold as much as self-sufficient. Your power is to carve order out of chaos. Disorder disturbs you, and you need to organize and control your surroundings. This means you occasionally take a strong hand in other people's lives. To you, it's not meddling but *handling* things better. You're oriented toward excellence and, therefore, assume leadership as naturally as you breathe in and out. Yet beneath your reserve is a sensitive and sympathetic person, and anyone who needs a strong shoulder to lean on needn't look farther than Capricorn.

Certainly, you do not deserve your reputation for being sober and gloomy. One of your more striking characteristics is a sense of humor. Your wit may be dry, incisive, but it is extremely funny and has a way of erupting when others least expect it.

As is your nature with everything in life, you are cautious and conservative with money. Chances are you will amass wealth during your lifetime (usually in later years), for you know how to make sound investments. In business, your success is due to painstaking preparation. The journey of ten thousand miles may begin with a single step, but you know you can't get anywhere unless you first know where you're going. You may not size up a situation as quickly as some, but this can be an advantage, for it means you won't heedlessly plunge in. Instead, you will research, examine what others have done before, and gather all relevant data. Only then, with a thorough understanding of the details, will you begin to move. And then you won't be stopped until you reach your goal.

You are not comfortable with ambiguity. You seek certainty and tend to see things in black and white. Emotional gray areas are troublesome, and you turn away from them. You form judgmental opinions based on surface impressions. To the unevolved Capricorn there is only one "right" way—which is his or her way. Proud of being a high-functioning achiever, you have little tolerance for others' frailty. Capricorn can be critical and close minded, and put value only in power and success.

Your basic concern is for security. That goal comes first, and you are usually materialistic. You can be spiteful toward those who stand in the way. You're deeply invested in your image and cannot bear showing to the world anything less than someone of merit and accomplishment. You will not forgive anyone who belittles or slights you. By the same token, you will repay favors done for you. Scorpios also go out of their way to repay a kindness, but in their case it is done out of a sense of gratitude and fidelity. With you, the motivation is pride that does not allow you to live comfortably under an obligation.

More than any other sign of the zodiac, Capricorns marry for money and prestige. In most relationships you must dominate, because when you are in control you do not feel vulnerable to another person's power. In small ways, you are continually testing the loyalty of those close to you. You are the loner of the zodiac but have a great need to be loved and appreciated. Unfortunately, you won't let this need be known—in fact, you are a master at concealing it.

Underneath the mask, you wear still other masks, and it can take a long time to discover the real you. To others you may appear aloof, indifferent, hard to reach because you are so self-contained. But the very elusiveness of your Capricorn personality can be hypnotically attractive. Like a riddle wrapped inside a sphinx, there seems to be a fascinating secret buried in your depths.

Anyone who cares enough to penetrate your shell of reserve will be greatly rewarded. Your affections and loyalty run deep, and you cherish and protect those you love. And you stick around when the going is toughest.

THE INNER YOU

You don't need anyone to convince you that life is serious business; you've known it all along. That's what keeps you anxiously asking yourself: Am I fulfilling my responsibilities? Am I achieving as much as I should? Am I self-reliant enough? You know you have the persistence and strength of purpose to reach your goals. But you also have a deep need to connect on an emotional level in your relationships so that you won't feel separated from those you care about. You worry about keeping all that's valuable to you—which includes relationships. Despite your intelligence and the fact that you're so determined, you often feel insecure. You're a bundle of conflicting emotions. You require discipline and order—chaos drives you crazy and makes you doubt yourself and what you're capable of. But maybe the gods meant for you to have some doubt; if you believed you're as powerful as you really are, you'd be impossible to live with!

HOW OTHERS SEE YOU

You're often seen as an irresistible force and an immovable object. People put you in charge because you're decisive—you're famous for having a great sense of realism. When others need a rational head in a crisis, they call on you. In personal relationships, some friends will stand in line to unload their problems on you; others avoid you because they think your outlook is too downbeat. Everyone agrees that it's difficult to divert you from your course when you've set a goal. Some people feel that in order to find the real you they have to strip away layers of secrecy, but most understand that your aloofness stems from a deep sense of personal privacy.

GUARD AGAINST: Being Merciless to Yourself

You are driven, to be sure, but when you keep this in balance with the rest of your life, you're a great achiever. The problem is you're exceedingly intense about fulfilling the tasks you've taken on. You put enormous pressure on yourself to steer an enterprise to completion, and you easily slip into addiction to work and joyless drudgery. You wrestle with guilty feelings and melancholia.

Each of the three Earth signs—Taurus, Virgo, and Capricorn—expresses its earth-quality differently. Taurus uses it to build something stable; Virgo gathers resources in order to serve. Capricorn pushes up out of the earth toward the sky. Its nature is to climb the mountain. In esoteric terms, Capricorn rules mastery over the physical world.

If you don't feel you're operating at peak performance, it strikes at the core of your self-esteem. You're your harshest critic. To your mind, unless you see an endeavor to a victorious result, you are a failure. You're determined to win the goal you were after. Usually, even this is not good enough. Basically, you're searching for approval you can never find on the outside because it can only come from yourself.

The issue is you try to live up to a rigid code, an image of yourself. You see yourself as *self*-created. You're the one who causes things to happen and who draws success to yourself. Often it's not enough to make it to the top; you need to find glory at the top. Anything less is shattering to your belief about yourself. The outer image you've created is very real to you—and, indeed, unless you're careful, you will lose your inner self and come to believe totally in your outer self.

YOUR GREATEST CHALLENGE:
To Feel Comfortable with Your Emotional Self

This is the part of you that you tend to stuff away. What you project is competence, efficiency, poise, and boldness. As an Earth sign, Capricorn operates most masterfully in the arena of the practical, pragmatic, substantial, and real. You gravitate toward ambitious schemes and daunting projects.

What's contradictory is that beneath your strong, authoritative manner and despite all the talents you display, you struggle with self-esteem. You're highly self-critical and deeply self-conscious. You're vulnerable and fear getting hurt. You work diligently to gain respect and approval from the outside, but not from the inside because you can't find it there. On a deep level, you don't approve of yourself and therefore try harder and harder to be superior in the public eye.

Yet your self-drive and self-control can become very distorted. Even from an early age you learned to hold yourself in check and react to events (especially painful ones) with a minimum display of emotion. You suppress your responses and turn to stone. Life may careen out of control, but you are in control. In spite of your truly profound ability to care, you maintain a level of coolness— and those around you quickly learn that you remain oblivious to problems with which you don't want to deal.

Another aspect to the Capricorn dichotomy between mind and heart, between outer self and inner self, is your fending off of people who try to get too close emotionally. You do have a few trusted friends whose loyalty you cherish—but in general you're not fond of anyone trying to break in and get near to your core. Your reaction is to disassociate from a person advancing toward you. Capricorn has a well-earned reputation for being private and aloof.

Still, your inner self yearns for intimacy, friendship, love, and affection, and your greatest challenge is to tap into your Capricorn courage to open your feelings and allow your vulnerability and sensitivity to be seen. Only by learning to be comfortable with your own emotions can you ever discover how loved you are by others.

Astrology gives us many tools in our lives to help manage our struggles and solve problems. One of these tools is to reach into your opposite sign in the zodiac—your polarity.

For you, Capricorn, this is Cancer, sign of foundations, family, childhood, roots, and the beginning of new growth. The sign of Cancer symbolizes the process of giving birth—mentally (as in creative pursuits), emotionally (as in forming and fostering relationships), and physically (as in biologically producing offspring). Cancer's ruler, the Moon, presides over the feminine principle (feelings, instinct, nurturing, creative work). Astrologically, the Moon represents all aspects of mothering and fertility; it is linked to memory, dreams, and the unconscious.

Like you, Cancer has great drive and magnetism. Capricorn and Cancer share an active intelligence, need for stability, belief in traditional values, and patient perseverance. But unlike you, Cancer is at home in the waters of emotion. Cancerians are in touch with their inner selves and creative imagination, known for their intuitive way of dealing with people. They are caregivers and creators. They have a special gift for being supportive to others and operate effectively in situations that resemble family dynamics. In the workplace, in the boardroom, socially, and in domestic life, Cancerians are at their best being part of a close-knit group. You, Capricorn, are far more the lone go-getter.

Both Capricorn and Cancer are Cardinal signs (the quality of initiating), and you both use this forward-pushing energy particularly to gain financial security. But Cancer is looking to create a downy nest of safety and comfort, whereas Capricorn wants to win success in the larger world. Your ambition is to achieve glory and respect; without even being aware of it, you seek to be in authority. You may have a number of associates but few intimates. Indeed, in your climb up the ladder, you tend to shed people who cease being useful.

Having to be unbeatable does put heavy pressure on you, and the stress of performing magnifies your darker Capricorn qualities. You can become ferociously obsessed, turn demanding and dictatorial. Your cold, unsympathetic demeanor distances you from others, which makes you feel ever lonelier.

The sad thing is you secretly struggle with self-esteem issues, and an all-important reason you strive to be thought well of is you need approval. Still, what you yearn for you push away. Intimacy is hard; you're not experienced in sharing and in emotional give-and-take. Yet you can ease the discomfort and, in fact, feel far less vulnerable by adopting some of Cancer's openness to relationships. Similarly to you, Cancer is self-protective and takes time learning to trust. But your relationship style is to make others live up to your expectations. Cancer's is to enter into unions as a giver and sharer.

Whether in business or personal life, you will find greater happiness in your associations by looking for what you can give instead of what you can get. This is not Pollyanna stuff; when your heart is open, you operate from a place of feeling rather than fearing. This banishes dark self-doubt and lets in the light of joy. Cancer's comfort in the emotional zone and willingness to let imagination loose are valuable lessons for closed Capricorn.

In turn, Cancer has many lessons to learn from you. Among the most priceless is your courage. You are not a quitter, and therefore you're able to triumph over all obstacles. Cancer tends to sidestep or hide away and could certainly find greater success by adopting your bold manner. At your core is a person who is real, substantial, and deep; you are born with wisdom. Psychologists would say Capricorn has the ability to "self-actualize"—inch by inch, you learn to stand tall in your own power. Indeed, this is a Capricorn lesson that *every* sign can learn from!

CAPRICORN IN LOVE

You may not show it, but you care a great deal about love. Deep in your inner core is an extravagant romantic who yearns to be swept away by passion. Yet you are also very private, aloof, restrained, and reticent about your feelings.

When you walk into a room, people know they're in the presence of someone distinctive. Class and elegance are hallmarks of your sign. People are attracted to your elusive reserve, drawn to the mystery they sense in you. Few recognize this as a cover for extremely powerful emotions.

Unlike those who are content to leave love to fate, Capricorn takes a hand in determining its own fate. You're the least likely of all the zodiacal signs to fall in love at first sight. Discriminating in your choice of lovers, you never give your love frivolously or capriciously and have no time to waste in silly flirtation. Love is a serious matter.

If a would-be lover doesn't measure up, you want this person out of your way. If there is someone who does interest you, you'll observe him or her from an emotional distance before moving closer. You take the time to get to know a person. Your most basic concern is for security, and you consider carefully the consequences of any emotional involvement before committing yourself. No one is going to hurt you if you can help it. You'd like a *guaranteed* relationship. Like all Earth signs (Taurus, Virgo, Capricorn), your deep-rooted sensuality flowers only when you feel safe.

If a person is set on winning you, he or she had better prepare for a long siege, for you're not easy to win. In a love partner, you want someone who will cherish and understand you, who won't ask you to relinquish your goals. You're also looking for a worthy mate for your self-image. If you're a Capricorn woman, you'd like a man with polish, intelligence, and a substantial bank account. If you're a man, you want an accomplished, gifted woman who will add style to your life and make a graceful impression socially.

Especially early on, Capricorns tend to be unlucky in love. They still have much to learn about relating, about give-and-take between *two* people. It's as if as a child you're imprinted with the role of the "ruler," and usually it takes the experience of ill-advised choices and heartbreak to teach lessons in how to love genuinely. In her first affairs, a Capricorn woman often becomes involved with younger men she can dominate. The Capricorn man enters early alliances as the authority figure who has the final word, and this brings on numerous problems in his relationships. In time, however, with Capricorn's great capacity for loyalty, you find your way into true intimacy—and always your emotional journey is about letting go of the fear of getting hurt.

When the ice melts, the flames leap up, and definitely Capricorn is known for passionate sexuality. This is strong glue in holding love relationships together, but here as well Capricorn must learn to handle the emotional volatility of sex. The Capricorn woman experiences conflict over being "swept away," and the Capricorn man may be lusty but totally insensitive. Both genders are uncomfortable giving over emotionally—the Capricorn woman because she feels both vulnerable and independent and the Capricorn man because he wants to retain final control.

Perhaps the difficult process of arriving at emotional serenity is best understood by looking at Capricorn's ruler, Saturn. This is the planet of seriousness and accomplishment, but its dark side is melancholia and inner loneliness. Many self-made Capricorns who are exceedingly smart and highly ambitious are also isolated and hampered emotionally. You were born knowing how to use your talents but needing to learn how to reach across the chasm of feeling cut off. Your greatest lesson is to find *self*-love. When you achieve this, magically you become free to love someone else.

At your best, Capricorn, you are magnetic, hypnotic, deep, generous, loyal, and devoted. The person who penetrates your shell and finds the vulnerable you will be rewarded by a lifetime of constancy. Capricorn is the sign of endurance, and this holds as true for the manner in which you love as for your enormous capacity for work. Your strength is your ability to commit yourself, and in love, you thrive in giving. Nothing can shake your protective instinct for the one you love. The core of your character is that you're steadfast and unswerving. You will stand by your mate when the going is toughest.

TIPS FOR THOSE WHO WANT TO
ATTRACT CAPRICORN

If Capricorns appear aloof at first, it's because they are calculating the risks of a new friendship.

They are quite willing to be your audience, so don't be afraid to take the initiative in conversation. A sure way to capture Capricorns' interest is to be amusing, for they are basically melancholy types who need an emotional lift. In addition, they respond to humor because their own dry wit surfaces when they feel comfortable.

They often try to mask their feelings because they are afraid of exposing too much of themselves. Never mind that their fears are unfounded; this is how they feel. Even at their most open, Capricorns will be pretty hard to fathom.

Capricorns are interested in art, music, and theater and are drawn to people who are intellectually stimulating. They prefer to talk of serious subjects. When they decide to state an opinion, listen as if you were hearing the Gettysburg Address for the first time. And don't come up with radical or far-out opinions. They shun unconventionality.

You can't go wrong getting a Capricorn something practical as a gift. Be sure it is of the best quality, not something gaudy or showy. Persons born under this sign appreciate luxury but are far too aware of the value of a dollar to respect anyone who splurges merely to make an impression. Books are always a good item, especially biographies, self-help books, well-researched historical novels, and books dealing with investments.

Tip: Always be on time. Time is money—and you know how Capricorns feel about that.

CAPRICORN'S EROGENOUS ZONES:
Tips for Those with a Capricorn Lover

Our bodies are very sensitive to the touch of another human being. The special language of touching is understood on a level more basic than speech. Each sign is linked to certain zones and areas of the body that are especially receptive and can receive sexual messages through touch. Many books and manuals have been written about lovemaking, but few pay attention to the unique knowledge of erogenous zones supplied by astrology. You can use astrology to become a better, more sensitive lover.

The special erotic area for Capricorn is the knees. Capricorn's slumbering passions are instantly awakened if you gently brush stroke, fondle, or kiss the area around the knees.

Either male or female Capricorns will be sexually stimulated by a sensual massage that starts in the small of the lower back. Use your fingertips or fingernails and stroke lightly, just touching the skin. Make long strokes from the lower back, down along the buttocks, the backs of the thighs, and on to the backs of the knees. Return that same way, but this time shorten the stroke. Keep shortening your featherlight strokes until they are concentrated around the back of the knees. A variation would be to use your tongue and lips in slow short circles on the skin around the knees.

The effect on Capricorn is volcanic!

CAPRICORN'S AMOROUS COMBINATIONS: YOUR LOVE PARTNERS

CAPRICORN AND ARIES

Both of you are Cardinal signs and are attracted by each other's dynamism and energy. It doesn't take long to become involved sexually—but even in bed there'll be arguments about money, friends, socializing, and who's boss. A major difference is that you won't make a move unless sure of winning, whereas Aries is headstrong and impulsive. You see Aries as having a completely unrealistic approach to life, and Aries feels weighed down by your heavy-handed practicality. Arguments never fade away, for both of you are strong willed and aggressive and need to dominate. You're very competitive with each other. Jealousy also raises its head because Aries's lively passions are likely to stray toward more fun-loving company, and you absolutely won't put up with disloyalty. Temperamentally and emotionally, this mating is better suited to an arena than to hearth and home.

CAPRICORN AND TAURUS

Taurus admires your strength of purpose, and you are delighted with Taurus's affectionate stability. Taurus is able to get through your aloof, cautious manner and give you the encouragement and responsiveness you need. You both have earthy, passionate natures, and sensual Taurus can tap the deep well of romanticism lying under your reserve. You are loyal and Taurus is devoted, so jealousy is not a problem. You also share interests and hobbies, enjoy nice possessions, and are home lovers. Your strongest bond is your shared valuing of money and security. You inspire each other's career goals, and as a working team you two can make money grow. You may need to watch that you don't get overly focused on work. The nice thing is Taurus makes you feel loved for who you are rather than how much money you earn. One union, strong and indivisible.

CAPRICORN AND GEMINI

You're drawn to Gemini's charm and fun-loving spirits, and Gemini is fascinated by your quiet intensity. You're both intelligent, and at the beginning you enjoy learning how each other's mind works. You'll also fall into a brief physical passion—but very soon discover you have nothing in common. Capricorn has a hard time holding the reins on excitable, flirtatious, wayward Gemini. You prize order, control, and stability, and approach life in a practical, determined manner. To you, life needs to be centered. Gemini is disorganized, high-strung, and erratic. It will take all your Capricorn patience to deal with a partner you consider capricious, extravagant, and scatterbrained. Also, Gemini's verbal quickness has a way of making you secretly feel inadequate. Neither of you is particularly sentimental, so whatever flamelets ignite at the beginning will quickly cool.

CAPRICORN AND CANCER

You two are opposites in the zodiac, and thus each can give what the other is short of. You can tap into Cancer's emotionalism, and Cancer can benefit from your sense of discipline. Certainly, you're sexually attracted to each other, for you both have deep passions. The problem is you'll need all the physical harmony you can find in the bedroom to offset the discordance you're likely to create everywhere else. Sensitive Cancer will resent the Capricorn domineering manner. You in turn aren't willing to put up with Cancer's endless emotional demands and damp, clingy behavior. Cancer's need for warmth will be frustrated by your aloof coolness. Both of you fear rejection, but Cancer's tendency is to withdraw and yours is to become tyrannical. However long this relationship lasts, Capricorn will be the dominant partner. The question is: Is this uneasy mix worth all the difficulties?

CAPRICORN AND LEO

Both of you are independent and have domineering personalities—so from the start your relationship is a struggle. Capricorn is ordered and organized, and you neither understand nor approve of Leo's exuberant impulsiveness. You cannot stand Leo's habit of leaping first and looking afterward, and you especially have zero tolerance for Leo's monumental ego and vanity. Meanwhile, extroverted Leo will be impatient with your secretive tendencies, finds you unimaginative, and thinks you're stingy with affection. Capricorn is too reserved to give Leo the adoration it needs, and proud Leo will not give in to Capricorn's domineering ways. Spendthrift Leo adores luxury, while Capricorn puts financial security above all else. To cap this mismatch, you both want to rule in the bedroom. You're an unpromising couple who'll find your way to a quick ending.

CAPRICORN AND VIRGO

You two are Earth signs with much in common. You're both committed to creating a secure life and making it run more efficiently. Virgo's neat orderly mind meshes well with Capricorn's self-discipline and capacity for hard work. Both of you take pride in your home, enjoy having a few close friends rather than many acquaintances, and admire each other's intellectual abilities. Both are dependable, conservative, understanding. Although Virgo tends to be a worrier, which can dampen your spirits, Virgo is an excellent helpmate for your Capricorn ambitions and will work right alongside you. There's no reason your duo shouldn't click— except in the bedroom, where Virgo's reticence needs a stronger push than reserved Capricorn likes to give. Neither of you finds it easy to be spontaneously affectionate. However, this is the only minus entry on a balance sheet full of pluses.

CAPRICORN AND LIBRA

Immediately, you're intrigued by magnetic Libra, and Libra is charmed by your slowly revealed passions. But when the bloom is off the rose, you find Libra too self-centered and unresponsive to your needs. Over the long term, Libra wants more excitement, romance, and beauty than Capricorn can provide. The problem is Capricorn and Libra are Cardinal signs whose initiating energies go in different directions. Libra's focus is on socializing and creativity, and yours is on work and security. You're not oriented toward parties and artistic pursuits, which are Libra's favorite activities. Capricorn prizes discipline and responsibility, and you find Libra altogether too frivolous and vain, and a spendthrift to boot. Libra turns restive and starts to look elsewhere. Throw in some Capricorn jealousy to keep the cauldron bubbling. A recipe for disaster.

CAPRICORN AND SCORPIO

What draws Capricorn and Scorpio together is intensity, though each of you has a different kind. Yours is concentrated on achievement, and Scorpio has fierce emotional intensity; still, the blending works. Sexually, Scorpio has a powerful eroticism that kindles your slumbering passions. Scorpio is the more imaginative lover, but Capricorn's stamina is a delightful match. Success in the bedroom opens up other areas of affection and sharing. Scorpio's possessiveness spells security to Capricorn; you understand it's a symptom of love. You two also work well as a team—Capricorn is highly organized and Scorpio has native shrewdness. Both prize discipline and accomplishment. Each is strong willed, and sometimes Scorpio's renowned temper comes up against your Capricorn stubbornness. Your battles will be royal, but so will your makings-up.

CAPRICORN AND SAGITTARIUS

At first, each of you might have something the other needs—such as the sparkle Sagittarius can add to your day, and the grounding you can provide for Sagittarius. Sagittarius's optimism has a way of cheering you and, in turn, Sagittarius is very drawn to your depth and self-containment. All too soon, though, your huge personality differences create discord. You become annoyed by Sagittarius's fickle attitude and total need for freedom without strings. Sagittarius is off on a myriad of pie-in-the-sky pursuits while you single-mindedly focus on what's important. Sagittarius is impetuous and has free-and-easy spending habits; you are serious-minded and a stay-at-home. Also, you sense you can't count on Sagittarius's loyalty through thick and thin, and you're frustrated by Sagittarius's nonchalance in love. The ties that bind are soon cut.

CAPRICORN AND CAPRICORN

You approve of people like yourself, so with you two there's no lack of mutual respect and regard. Both of you are cautious, reserved personalities who work hard and love to save money. Major plusses are the friendship, loyalty, and trust you share. But even compatibility can sometimes be dull; as partners, you're okay but not too much fun. You're well-matched sexually, for you both have strong libidos, but in other areas you encourage each other's tendencies to be gloomy and pessimistic. Neither of you can relax or let down your hair—each really needs someone with more levity and liveliness. Love travels an almost imperceptibly downhill road. The emotional storyline is that each has to settle for less than you hoped for at the beginning. Ultimately, your relationship becomes more of a power struggle than a romance.

CAPRICORN AND AQUARIUS

You're intrigued by Aquarius's mental quickness and even more so by its unorthodox sexual proclivities. All too quickly, however, Aquarius loses erotic interest. Indeed, a key problem in this relationship is that Aquarius lives in its mind and is constantly into the next new thing. The result is you find Aquarius far too unpredictable, and certainly eccentric. Aquarius is future oriented, whereas you deal with what's at hand. Your approach to life quickly irritates adventurous Aquarius. Aquarius believes in self-expression; Capricorn believes in self-discipline. Especially, Aquarius's impersonal attitude makes you uneasy—Aquarius is somewhat a rover, while you prefer home and hearth. Freedom-loving Aquarius won't stay bound for long to earnest, staid Capricorn. However, you two should like each other, and love can turn into friendship.

CAPRICORN AND PISCES

You, Capricorn, provide ballast for Pisces's drifting dreaminess, and you supply the stability that Pisces needs and admires. And there's nothing you like better than being admired. In the boudoir you're captain, but Pisces is a willing crew. Pisces's taste for the bizarre may even influence your more conventional passions. Emotionally, Pisces's generous affections and Capricorn's strong sense of loyalty combine to make each of you feel safe and protected. You also make a good business team, for Pisces has the dream and you have the follow-through. The real key to your success as a couple and partnership is that Pisces is highly adaptable, and therefore falls in with your steadfast approach. True, a part of each of you will always be a stranger to the other, but your relationship is a felicitous match of two very different people who meet each other's needs.

YOUR CAPRICORN CAREER PATH

A career is what Capricorn is born for. This doesn't mean you have to be rich and famous, or be a president, celebrity, corporate executive, or captain of industry. It means you are fulfilled by accomplishing. Whether your occupation is singing on the Broadway stage or parenting a child, you are happiest when you execute a job well.

In astrology, the sign of Capricorn represents the Midheaven, the top of the zodiac wheel closest to the stars. Your sign therefore is linked to the concept of high achievement. In your career, you merge determination (your Earth quality) with initiative (your Cardinal quality)—and, like the Goat (your symbol), you deliberately, persistently, patiently keep on climbing.

Your patience is definitely a great boon to your career. Time is your friend, not your enemy. People envy you because you seem to have it all, but you *earn* everything you have. You're willing to put in the time and the work.

Nor are you a winging-it type of person. You are fond of structure—structure of time, plans, organization. These are your building blocks. You tend to move conservatively, weigh an action, and then purposefully pursue your goal. It's this purposeful action combined with your visionary quality that puts you in the stratosphere of success.

Your professional magic is your fusion of the real and practical with wonderful aesthetic gifts, and all of it fueled by your persistence. You do the basic hard work, and then you're willing to take your endeavor into realms others haven't inhabited yet.

You see the possibility in a project, and what you see goes way beyond what others envision. Add the fact you have clear intention—you stay with your vision and step-by-step turn it into a reality. Obstacles don't deter you. Indeed, problem solving seems to be a Capricorn sport. You enjoy trying different solutions to making something work.

You're best suited to a career where you can take charge and apply your own high standards. These include science, teaching, journalism, the legal arena, and politics. You are also very much at home with money; financial advising, banking, insurance, and accounting are open fields for you. Capricorn is a builder, and you're gifted at architecture and engineering. Many Capricorns have musical ability or are drawn to publishing, museum work, and art collecting. In business, you tend to rise to positions of leadership and often find the most satisfaction in running your own company.

Capricorn is the sign of authority. You sincerely believe authority carries the responsibility of superior knowledge, and you place a high value on authority figures. Having the approval of someone you admire is a tremendous motivator. Usually, when starting out, Capricorn finds a father figure or mentor who opens doors and assists in learning the early ropes.

Yet you need to be careful of confusing approval because of your achievement in work with approval and love for you as a human being. You feel you are what you do—and the more perfectly you do it, the more perfect you are. Your sense of worth is tied up with performing well. This can lead to your becoming overprotective of your position and fearful of losing it. You grow suspicious of "enemies" around you who want to grab what belongs to you. To the unevolved Capricorn, the most valuable things in life are status, position, and material things. Because of extreme effort and discipline, the Capricorn has acquired these things and will not let anyone take them away.

At issue is your ego, which is at once insecure and overinflated. Often your drive to the top is compensation for a weak sense of self (one of your most hidden secrets). If you can win applause and respect from others, you convince yourself you're worthy. At the same time, your ego demands self-aggrandizement. You are important and admirable, and in this state of mind, your opinions are the truth and what you think is the right way. You brook no opposition.

Still, Capricorn has the capacity to move past a base desire for power, to move past the superficial. At heart, you're a giver—and the giving of yourself is truly the thing that fulfills you. In your work, you bring your total self to what you do, and no one goes further than you in committing yourself. Your gifts are unlike anyone else's. You have a quick and analytical mind matched with an instinct for handling people. You create your own opportunities and are unafraid to take on impossible challenges. To you, having a career means responsibility and results, and you have sheer endurance. Tenacious and hardworking, you push ahead, building, gaining, keeping. You're a superachiever—and you deserve all the accolades you win!

CAPRICORN AND HEALTH:
ADVICE FROM ASTROLOGY

"Keep moving" is your health mantra, for you have a tendency to stiffen up, especially as time goes by. Capricorn has problems with knees and joints. You're prone to developing arthritis, and susceptible to injuries and ailments affecting ligaments, tendons, and cartilage. To stay flexible you need regular exercise that is fun and relaxing. Exercise is also a mood lifter, and since Capricorn can suffer from dark doldrums and depression, you definitely need body movement to lift your spirits. Your planetary ruler, Saturn, governs skin, bones, and teeth, which you must safeguard. Practice good oral hygiene and have regular dental checkups, and take care of your sensitive skin. The keys to your good health are to keep your body flexible and look after the well-being of your teeth, bones, joints, and knees.

Advice and useful tips about health are among the most important kinds of information that astrology provides. Health and well-being are of paramount concern to human beings. Love, money, or career takes second place, for without good health we cannot enjoy anything in life.

Astrology and medicine have had a long marriage. Hippocrates (born around 460 B.C.), the Greek philosopher and physician who is considered the father of medicine, said, "A physician without a knowledge of astrology has no right to call himself a physician." Indeed, up until the eighteenth century, the study of astrology and its relationship to the body was very much a part of a doctor's training. When a patient became ill, a chart was immediately drawn up. This guided the doctor in both diagnosis and treatment, for the chart would tell when the crisis would come and what medicine would help. Of course, modern Western doctors no longer use astrology to treat illness. However, astrology can still be a useful tool in helping to understand and maintain our physical well-being.

THE PART OF THE BODY RULED BY CAPRICORN

Each sign of the zodiac governs a specific part of the body. These associations date back to the beginning of astrology. Curiously, the part of the body that a sign rules is in some ways the strongest and in other ways the weakest area for natives of that sign.

Your sign of Capricorn rules the bones, joints, knees, and teeth. Capricorns are known for their beautiful bone structure and stately carriage. Capricorn women often have a striking angular beauty, especially in their facial bones, which makes them very photogenic. Both men and women have strong constitutions, are vigorous and enduring, and are capable of withstanding stress and illness. Your health seems to get better as you get older. Along with Leo and Sagittarius, Capricorn is noted for longevity.

Your bones, joints, and knees, however, are vulnerable to accidents, fractures, bumps, bruises, and cuts. Your knees tire more easily than other parts of your body. Many Capricorns complain of a bothersome trick knee and of bone aches throughout the body. Chief dangers are rheumatism, arthritis, neuralgia, stiff joints, and orthopedic problems.

Your ruling planet, Saturn, holds sway over the gallbladder, spleen, bones, skin, and teeth. Capricorns usually have good-looking teeth, but they require a great deal of care and dentistry. Your skin tends to be dry and sensitive.

You're inclined to be introspective and moody, and many Capricorns suffer from depression. Ill health and indefinable aches and pains can be brought on by negative emotions. Worry drains your energy and spirits. Capricorn tends to have trouble with the demon drink.

In general, however, yours is among the healthiest, sturdiest signs. You remain active and agile into old age—and in fact, don't seem to age at all. It's been noted that Capricorns look old when they're young, and young when they're old.

DIET AND HEALTH TIPS FOR CAPRICORN

A diet high in protein and calcium is a must in order to keep your bones, skin, and teeth in prime condition. Capricorns tend to do things in excess. You overwork, skip meals, then eat too much at one time. You should go easy on the highly seasoned and spicy food you are fond of, for it causes intestinal upsets. A gloomy Capricorn will seek solace in alcohol, which you do not handle well.

Capricorn's cell salt* is calcium phosphate, which is the most important element in bone formation and composition of the skel-

*Cell salts (also known as tissue salts) are mineral compounds found in human tissue cells. These minerals are the only substances our cells cannot produce by themselves. The life of cells is relatively short, and the creation of new cells depends on the presence of these minerals.

eton. Lack of calcium phosphate causes rickets, misshapen bones, spinal curvature, tooth disorders, and pains in the joints. Foods rich in this mineral that Capricorn needs are oranges, lemons, figs, celery, cabbage, kale, dandelion greens, spinach, broccoli, corn, peas, potatoes, walnuts, almonds, whole wheat, oats, and brown rice. You should include in your diet every day a fresh raw salad, fresh fruits and vegetables, lean protein, fish, eggs, and whole-grain breads. You need lots of calcium foods, such as cheese, buttermilk, and yogurt. You tend to get into a rut about food likes and dislikes and often eat the same things every day. You should try to vary your diet with different vegetables, fruit, meat, and fish.

You're bothered by dry, itchy skin, especially in wintertime. Oils from apricots, sesame, and almond are soothing and replenishing, and you should use a moisturizer and sunscreen on a daily basis. Drinking plenty of water will keep your skin clear and plump. Eating chocolate and refined sugar is bad for your skin. And never overdo when sunbathing, for your skin will quickly take on the patina of old cracked leather.

Other tips: Keep warm and wrapped up in cold, damp weather. If you surround yourself with color, flowers, soothing music, and pleasant people, your mood will lighten. You should strive for good posture, sit up straight, and loosen your gait. Warm baths, moderate exercise, and long walks in the country are very relaxing.

THE DECANATES AND CUSPS OF CAPRICORN

Decanate and *cusp* are astrological terms that subdivide your Sun sign. These subdivisions further define and emphasize certain qualities and character traits of your Sun sign, Capricorn.

WHAT IS A DECANATE?

Each astrological sign is divided into three parts, and each part is called a *decanate* or a *decan* (the terms are used interchangeably).

The word comes from the Greek word *dekanoi*, meaning "ten days apart." The Greeks took their word from the Egyptians, who divided their year into 360 days.* The Egyptian year had twelve months of thirty days each, and each month was further divided into three sections of ten days each. It was these ten-day sections the Greeks called *dekanoi*.

---

*The Egyptians soon found out that a 360-day year was inaccurate and so added on five extra days. These were feast days and holidays, and not counted as real days.

Astrology still divides the zodiac into decanates. There are twelve signs in the zodiac, and each sign is divided into three decanates. You might picture each decanate as a room. You were born in the sign of Capricorn, which consists of three rooms (decanates). In which room of Capricorn were you born?

The zodiac is a 360-degree circle. Each decanate is ten degrees of that circle, or about ten days long, since the Sun moves through the zodiac at approximately the rate of one degree per day. (This is not exact because not all of our months contain thirty days.)

The decanate of a sign does not change the basic characteristics of that sign, but it does refine and individualize the sign's general characteristics. If you were born, say, in the second decanate of Capricorn, it does not change the fact you are a Capricorn. It does indicate that you have somewhat different and special characteristics from those Capricorn people born in the first decanate or the third decanate.

Finally, each decanate has a specific planetary ruler, sometimes called a subruler because it does not usurp the overall rulership of your sign. The subruler can only enhance and add to the distinct characteristics of your decanate. For example, your entire sign of Capricorn is ruled by Saturn, but the second decanate of Capricorn is subruled by Venus. The influence of Venus, the subruler, combines with the overall authority of Saturn to make the second decanate of Capricorn unlike any other in the zodiac.

FIRST DECANATE OF CAPRICORN

December 22 through December 31
Keyword: Responsibility

Constellation: Corona Australis, the Southern Crown, garland of the gods. The constellation symbolizes commitment to knowledge.

Planetary Subruler: Saturn

Saturn, planet of discipline, is both your ruler and subruler, which gives you a serious mien and a talent for handling responsibility. You are precise and orderly and generally don't trust others to look after details. When you undertake a task, you complete it to the best of your ability. Once you've set your mind on a goal, you are relentless and determined. There is a quiet force to your personality; other people are always aware of your presence. You are both subtle and aggressive, and you have an instinct for knowing how far you can push. Ambition usually motivates you, for you are never content to be an underling. Love brings out your affectionate and demonstrative nature. When aroused, you are a passionate person.

SECOND DECANATE OF CAPRICORN

January 1 through January 10

Keyword: Fairness

Constellation: Lyra, the Harp, formed by the god Mercury from a tortoiseshell. Lyra symbolizes harmony.

Planetary Subruler: Venus

Venus, planet of love, softens Saturn's stern influence and gives a gentleness and serenity to your personality. People respond to your warmth and charm. Venus here also indicates an interest in beauty and design, and perhaps some creative ability. In your work, you are practical and persistent. You are a doer who does not waste precious time. You enjoy periods of solitude to read, think, explore news subjects. Possibly, you carry on a large correspondence, for you write well. Travel holds fascination for you. Your lover, family, and friends take first place in your heart; you are devoted to their wants and needs. You are reticent about your feelings. Love is a deep emotion, and you don't readily speak of it.

THIRD DECANATE OF CAPRICORN

January 11 through January 19
Keyword: Honor
Constellation: Draco, the Dragon, the "seeing one" who guarded the Golden Apples. The Dragon symbolizes observation and intuition.
Planetary Subruler: Mercury

Mercury, planet of mental energy, adds impetus to the discipline of Saturn. You have a quick intellect and flexibility of character that allows you to adapt to different people and situations. When you give your word, you stick to it; you treat others fairly and with respect. Friends and admirers are drawn to your spiritual nature. You are an idealist and a dreamer, but when motivated, you are also an indefatigable worker. Money and material comforts are important to you, and you usually quickly spot where your best financial interests lie. You are a person of deep desires, though this may not be apparent on the outside. Life is often marked by a struggle to fulfill your inner needs.

WHAT IS A CUSP?

A cusp is the point at which a new astrological sign begins.* Thus, the cusp of Capricorn means the point at which Capricorn begins. (The word comes from the Latin word *cuspis*, meaning "point.")

When someone speaks of being "born on the cusp," that person is referring to a birth time at or near the beginning or the end of an astrological sign. For example, if you were born on January 19, you were born on the cusp of Aquarius, the sign that begins on January 20. Indeed, depending on what year you were born, your birth time might even be in the first degree of Aquarius. People born on the very day a sign begins or ends are often confused about what sign they really are—a confusion made more complicated by the fact that the Sun does not move into or out of a sign at *exactly* the same moment (or even day) each year. There are slight time differences from year to year. Therefore, if you are a Capricorn born on December 22 or January 19, you'll find great clarity consulting a computer chart that tells you exactly where the Sun was at the very moment you were born.

As for what span of time constitutes being born on the cusp, the astrological community holds various opinions. Some astrologers claim cusp means being born only within the first two days or last two days of a sign (though many say this is too narrow a time frame). Others say it can be as much as within the first ten days or last ten days of a sign (which many say is too wide an interpretation). The consensus is that you were born on the cusp if your birthday is within the first *five* days or last *five* days of a sign.

*In a birth chart, a cusp is also the point at which an astrological House begins.

The question hanging over cusp-born people is "What sign am I really?" They feel they straddle the border of two different countries. To some extent, this is true. If you were born on the cusp, you're under the influence of both signs. However, much like being a traveler leaving one country and crossing into another, you must actually *be* in one country—you can't be in two countries at the same time. One sign is always a stronger influence, and that sign is almost invariably the sign that the Sun was actually in (in other words, your Sun sign). The reason I say "almost" is that in rare cases a chart may be so heavily weighted with planets in a certain sign that the person more keenly feels the influence of that specific sign.

For example, I have a client who was born in the late evening on January 19. On that evening, the Sun was leaving Capricorn and entering Aquarius. At the moment of her birth, the Sun was still in Capricorn, so technically speaking she is a Capricorn. However, the Sun was only a couple hours away from being in Aquarius, and this person has the Moon, Mercury, and Venus all in Aquarius. She has always felt like an Aquarian and always behaved as an Aquarian.

This, obviously, is an unusual case. Generally, the Sun is the most powerful planetary influence in a chart. Even if you were born with the Sun on the very tip of the first or last degree of Capricorn, Capricorn is your Sun sign—and this is the sign you will most feel like.

Still, the influence of the approaching sign or of the sign just ending is present, and you will probably sense that mixture in yourself.

BORN DECEMBER 22 THROUGH DECEMBER 26

You are Capricorn with Sagittarius tendencies. Underneath your practical and sometimes unemotional approach, you have a kind and loving heart. People instinctively rely on your integrity. You do not betray their confidences and are a sympathetic listener. There is an adventurous quality to you; you like to travel and to explore new places and ideas. Even though you are conservative and cautious in your judgments, you are always willing to examine another point of view. You often pick up unspoken signals from others because of your keen sensitivity.

BORN JANUARY 15 THROUGH JANUARY 19

You are Capricorn with Aquarius tendencies. You are a deep person who possesses insight and vision, but you are also generous and fun loving and like to be in the company of people. You enjoy entertaining and the "good life," and may be known as an excellent host or hostess. Success is likely working with the public. In general, you look on the positive side, but when things go wrong, you are only able to see the negative. Your loyalty is unshakable, and you are always ready to help someone you love. In romance, you tend to settle for less than you deserve.

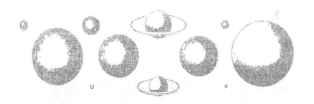

YOUR SPECIAL DAY OF BIRTH

DECEMBER 22

You have a powerful effect on people and are more innovative than many Capricorns. You trust your taste and will venture into a far-fetched project. You're lucky with money but, in love, need to look past the surface image into the other person's heart.

DECEMBER 23

You're outspoken and impatient, though you see yourself as a pussycat. It's just that you want to do your thing without people getting in your way. You do have a sensitive heart and in love can be quite impulsive. As you mature, you will find deep emotional serenity.

DECEMBER 24

Brash and bright, you also have Capricorn stolidity. You combine steel and softness. Your day of birth surrounds you with magic:

You'll always be rescued if you need it. Especially, you're destined to find the love partner who perfectly matches your tenderness.

DECEMBER 25

You're highly intelligent and, because of your one-of-a-kind opinions, known as an eccentric. Being a Christmas baby means you're gifted with future-vision that you should always trust. In love, you have honorable principles but also a flirtatious streak.

DECEMBER 26

A special zip to your personality gives you great people allure. You have practical ingenuity and are a keen observer of others' behavior. You also have an instinct for financial investing. In love, you're a bit of rebel and make romantic choices that surprise others.

DECEMBER 27

People find you fascinating, for you're extremely gifted and also very caring. In all your decisions, it would pay you to listen to your inner wisdom about yourself. In love, you're truthful and loyal and surprisingly sensitive to what your lover thinks of you.

DECEMBER 28

You have tremendous inner strength and make everything you do look easy. Indeed, people think you're superhuman for how much you can handle at once. In your work, you're a powerhouse, and in love, you have the rare ability to create joy and calmness in your relationships.

DECEMBER 29

It's hard to captivate you, for you're smarter than most and you bore easily. However, creative work does galvanize your innovative thinking, and friendships spark your gregarious nature. In love, your heart usually rules; you need to watch a tendency toward self-sacrifice.

DECEMBER 30

You are versatile and entertaining, and people enjoy conversing with you. Early on you may have trouble fixing on a career path, but the unusual work for which you're destined will arise out of trying many things. As for finding true love, this too will arrive unexpectedly.

DECEMBER 31

You're blessed with determination and a methodical mind, and you will carve out a very individual career path. You're skilled in communicating. Those not in your immediate circle don't realize the depth of your devotion, but your lover knows how protective you are.

JANUARY 1

Because you're a dominant personality, your riotous sense of humor is unexpected. You have a knack for charming the public and in groups tend to lead. In love, you have a jealous, possessive streak; be careful not to let this drive away someone who is true to you.

JANUARY 2

Undercurrents are hidden beneath your surface. To the world you're fun loving and playful, yet you're a deep thinker and exceptionally brilliant. You need space to be a creator. In love, you tend to settle for less than you're worthy of, but in time you learn to honor yourself.

JANUARY 3

You have unusual allure. You draw people to you; even strangers instinctively trust you. You're more creative than many Capricorns, and destined for imaginative work. Romantically, you go through early struggle and then, as you blossom, find everlasting love.

JANUARY 4

You have a fine mind and inner passion—and both are ignited by new ventures. You're a builder and strategist, and also an artist. Romantic affairs bring out your exuberance, and if you can learn to take a less controlling approach, you'll always be happy in love.

JANUARY 5

Though you worry about your imperfections, people see you as a fixed point in a changing world. You are ambitious and brilliant and must learn to make yourself a priority. In love, you tend to take the role of "rescuer" but are far better off with a strong partner.

JANUARY 6

You have imagination and outstanding ability in an area you can carve out as your own. You're gifted at fostering relationships and can make money in joint ventures. The only caution is in love—here you must not settle for a partner less talented or smart.

JANUARY 7

You're bright, chatty, and quick thinking, yet you also struggle with insecurity. Work keeps you sane, so concentrate on a career that expresses who you are. You have a sensitive heart, and because of your vulnerability, romance can be perplexing. Be sure you speak the truth.

JANUARY 8

You're polished and elegant, and seem as if you were born into money. But it's your superior intelligence that makes you classy. You're exceptionally suited for work in which you advise or direct others. In love, you're passionate and affectionate, and often too kindhearted.

JANUARY 9

Beneath your peaceable exterior you have a warrior spirit. You express yourself vividly, have a flair for performing, and excel in situations where you're righting a wrong. Romantic attachments spring up quickly, but the one that lasts forever will begin slowly.

JANUARY 10

Your great asset in relationships and business is your understanding of the human psyche. You also have a sharp, analytical eye for financial opportunity. In love, you're an idealist, but be careful about falling in love with an ideal and not the real person.

JANUARY 11

You're an individualist who stands out from the crowd and has the talent for stardom. But you're easily discouraged and need to work on your persistence. You do best not having to answer to others. In love, you look for magic, and having to face reality is often painful.

JANUARY 12

Though you're a practical realist, you have a poetic side you show when you feel safe. Emotionally, you're caring and wholehearted, yet you can seem detached and hard to please. The secret to finding serenity is to stop worrying what other people think.

JANUARY 13

When you want to attain a goal, you're dedicated and disciplined; otherwise, you're fonder of the easy life. You have sweet charm and keen intuition, and people seek out your friendship. Your heart is hungry for passionate love, and you'll experience it more than once.

JANUARY 14

You're a detective and psychologist, and little slips by your observant eye. This will always be helpful in your career, for it gives you an edge working with people. You're a flirtatious romantic, but your true happiness is found in a committed love partnership.

JANUARY 15

You're sentimental and self-sacrificing, but because you're also assertive, you have protective armor. In your work, you need challenge; choose carefully so that your brilliant mind is stimulated. In love, you show true devotion, yet you also need space of your own.

JANUARY 16

You have an artistic temperament and the spirit of an adventurer. You're the one who rides out into the world to help others and fix problems. You have a golden heart and deserve the best—in love especially, be sure to link up with someone honorable.

JANUARY 17

You're a thinker and talker, a collector of facts, organized but messy. Your contradictions make you delightful. You may experience romantic disappointment, but when you learn to be less demanding (which you don't see when you're young), you'll find your soulmate.

JANUARY 18

Your quicksilver responses (understanding of facts, sense of humor, etc.) endear you to others. You're talented at putting together the right people socially and in business. Romantically, you tend not to make the first move until you're sure, but then your passions explode.

JANUARY 19

You're both elegant and cuddly—you have a cool-warm quality. In your work, this connects you to those who support you and keeps away the others. In love, you have deep values that occasionally war with passing fancies. In the end, you'll choose the lover who gives you security.

YOU AND CHINESE ASTROLOGY

With Marco Polo's adventurous travels in A.D. 1275, Europeans learned for the first time of the great beauty, wealth, history, and romance of China. Untouched as they were by outside influences, the Chinese developed their astrology along different lines from other ancient cultures, such as the Egyptians, Babylonians, and Greeks in whom Western astrology has its roots. Therefore, the Chinese zodiac differs from the zodiac of the West. To begin with, it is based on a lunar cycle rather than Western astrology's solar cycle. The Chinese zodiac is divided into twelve years, and each year is represented by a different animal—the rat, ox, tiger, rabbit, dragon, snake, horse, goat, monkey, rooster, dog, and pig. The legend of the twelve animals is that when Buddha lay on his deathbed, he asked the animals of the forest to come and bid him farewell. These twelve were the first to arrive. The cat, as the story goes, is not among the animals because it was napping and couldn't be bothered to make the journey. (In some Asian countries, however, such as Vietnam, the cat replaces the rabbit.)

Like Western astrology in which the zodiac signs have different characteristics, each of the twelve Chinese animal years assigns character traits specific to a person born in that year. For example, the Year of the Rat confers honesty and an analytical mind, whereas the Year of the Monkey grants charm and quick ability to take advantage.

Here are descriptions for Capricorn for each Chinese animal year.

Important Note: If you are a Capricorn born in January, you are the Chinese sign of what would seem to be the previous year to your birth. The reason is that the Asian year is lunar. Our Western year always begins on January 1, but the Lunar New Year begins on the second new moon after the winter solstice. This means it can begin anywhere from very late in January to middle February. Many Capricorns read that their year of birth is a certain animal sign and don't realize that that Lunar Year did not begin until after their birthday.

For example, a Capricorn born in January 1981 might assume he or she was born in the Year of the Rooster. But the 1981 Year of the Rooster did not begin until February 5, and therefore the January Capricorn was actually born in the Year of the Monkey.

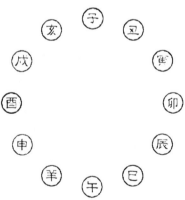

Years of the Rat

1900	1960	2020	2080
1912	1972	2032	2092
1924	1984	2044	
1936	1996	2056	
1948	2008	2068	

(Note: January Capricorns born in any of the above years are natives of the Year of the Pig.)

Unlike in the West, where the rat is shunned, the Asian Rat is loved for its courage, creativity, quick wit, and devastating charm. The Rat is known for superior adaptability. Rat qualities of sharp intuition and good judgment blend with Capricorn drive to create an achiever. As a brilliant Capricorn Rat, you see the big picture yet don't miss the details. You are inquisitive, can store away useful information, and are fast on your feet in a crisis. Those who are jealous of how enterprising you are say you're an opportunist. It's true you're quick to spot opportunity, and you can be meddling and critical. You're also a bit tight with your money though surprisingly generous to those you care for. You have sparkling sex appeal and are at your best in love. You put the happiness of your mate ahead of yours. Compatible partners are born in the Years of the Monkey, Pig, Rat, and Snake.

IF YOU ARE CAPRICORN BORN IN THE YEAR OF THE OX

Years of the Ox

1901	1961	2021	2081
1913	1973	2033	2093
1925	1985	2045	
1937	1997	2057	
1949	2009	2069	

(Note: January Capricorns born in any of the above years are natives of the Year of the Rat.)

Contrary to the plodding ox of the West, the Chinese Ox is elegant, courteous, gifted, and erudite. The Ox is the Chinese sign of authority and stability. Ox determination and resolve doubles Capricorn's sense of purpose. Plus, as a Capricorn Ox, you have extra imagination and an innovative outlook, and so you follow an off-the-beaten-track career path. You're an individualist with superior wisdom about the way the world works. At times you can be overbearing and impatient, and prissy in your methodical ways. You may seem unemotional but, in fact, are filled with passion—for new learning, the creative arts, good food, and sex. You're deeply sensual, which can lead to unhappiness in love when your physical appetites clash with your emotional promises. Compatible partners are born in the Years of the Rabbit, Rooster, Monkey, Pig, and Snake.

IF YOU ARE CAPRICORN BORN IN THE YEAR OF THE TIGER

Years of the Tiger

1902	1962	2022	2082
1914	1974	2034	2094
1926	1986	2046	
1938	1998	2058	
1950	2010	2070	

(Note: January Capricorns born in any of the above years are natives of the Year of the Ox.)

The Tiger is revered in Asia, for it symbolizes the power of faith. Certainly you demonstrate that faith can take you in unexplored directions. The Year of the Tiger confers daring, and this added to your Capricorn industriousness creates a high-flying type of personality. You're courageous and hugely generous, and a swirl of excitement surrounds you. Restless and passionate, you keep moving toward a larger goal, the undiscovered thing, the new place that will make you happy. Beware of spinning your wheels on something unworkable or dissipating your energies by taking on too much at once. Love partners don't always understand your inner needs, and at times you feel lonely. A special soulmate will fill this void. Yet you're a romantic who can be hurt, so you must choose wisely when it comes to marriage. Compatible partners are born in the Years of the Rabbit, Dog, Dragon, Monkey, Tiger, and Pig.

IF YOU ARE CAPRICORN BORN IN THE YEAR OF THE RABBIT

Years of the Rabbit

1903	1963	2023	2083
1915	1975	2035	2095
1927	1987	2047	
1939	1999	2059	
1951	2011	2071	

(Note: January Capricorns born in any of the above years are natives of the Year of the Tiger.)

The Asian Rabbit (or, in countries such as Vietnam, the Cat) is refined, theatrical, and delightfully imaginative. The Rabbit's graceful intelligence and flair for communicating infuse your Capricorn steadfastness, creating a dominating personality swathed in charm. You have a way of making a person feel you care particularly for him or her. Your instinct for spotting talent and putting the right people together ensures career success. Also, as a Capricorn Rabbit, you have extra resolve, for you're determined to feather your own nest so you'll be secure. You dislike conflict and tend to slip away when emotions are fraught. But when it comes to romance, you have extraordinary sexual allure. You attract creative, exotic, avant-garde types. Ultimately, though, what you want most will be true commitment. Compatible partners are born in the Years of the Goat, Dog, Dragon, Snake, Horse, and Monkey.

IF YOU ARE CAPRICORN BORN IN THE YEAR OF THE DRAGON

Years of the Dragon

1904	1964	2024	2084
1916	1976	2036	2096
1928	1988	2048	
1940	2000	2060	
1952	2012	2072	

(Note: January Capricorns born in any of the above years are natives of the Year of the Rabbit.)

The Asian Dragon, lauded in legend and mythology, symbolizes the realization of dreams. The Year of the Dragon sweeps out the old and opens the way to change. Chinese revere the Dragon, for it delivers good fortune. Dragon courage and charisma—and a rebel spirit—combine with Capricorn authority, giving you a super start in life. By focusing your talents and determination, you can get whatever you desire. People find you irresistible. Unlike many Capricorns, you have an open sunniness that makes others rush in to support you. You do need friendship, for your heart is loving. Because your interests are eclectic, you're sometimes thought an eccentric—but don't be afraid to strike out on new paths. Capricorn Dragon's destiny is to do work that takes you into untried areas. In love, you're an over-the-top romantic, passionately sexual, and sometimes too possessive. Compatible partners are born in the Years of the Rabbit, Goat, Monkey, Snake, and Tiger.

IF YOU ARE CAPRICORN BORN IN THE YEAR OF THE SNAKE

E

Years of the Snake

1905	1965	2025	2085
1917	1977	2037	2097
1929	1989	2049	
1941	2001	2061	
1953	2013	2073	

(Note: January Capricorns born in any of the above years are natives of the Year of the Dragon.)

The Asian Snake is treasured for its link to the Goddess of Beauty and the Sea and for being a good omen. The Snake is subtle, elegant, fluent of speech, and extremely magnetic. Born in the Year of the Snake, you have a radiance that captivates others. Snake creativity unites with Capricorn intelligence, making you successful at anything you're passionate about. You're good at business because you add an extra element that appeals to the public. Some say you're clairvoyant; certainly you're intuitive, and you use your sixth sense to sniff out financial opportunity. At times you exhibit a selfish streak. You're a real romantic charmer but are also complicated emotionally. You have a hidden melancholic side. You collect admirers rather casually, then suddenly fall desperately in love, which leads to tempestuous scenes. Compatible partners are born in the Years of the Rabbit, Rooster, Dragon, Horse, Ox, and Rat.

IF YOU ARE CAPRICORN BORN IN THE YEAR OF THE HORSE

Years of the Horse

1906	1966	2026	2086
1918	1978	2038	2098
1930	1990	2050	
1942	2002	2062	
1954	2014	2074	

(Note: January Capricorns born in any of the above years are natives of the Year of the Snake.)

The Horse is majestic and masterful, and so powerful that in Asia pregnancies are planned around a Horse year. The Horse symbolizes superiority, triumph, and a life of unusual feats. The Year of the Horse always promotes striking out on one's own—and this plus the confidence and fast-paced energy of the Horse unite with Capricorn ambition, resulting in a formidable *doer*. As a child, you may have felt like an awkward misfit, but Capricorn Horse soon blossoms into a force of nature. Your career is marked by exploits—breaking new ground, handling work others have never thought of. Because of your fierce independence, it never occurs to you something is impossible. You're very receptive to others but also highly resistant to being pinned down or put in a pigeonhole. In love, you're devoted. Many seek your attention because you're so attractive, but when you give your heart, you're exclusively faithful. Compatible partners are born in the Years of the Rabbit, Rooster, Goat, Horse, and Snake.

IF YOU ARE CAPRICORN BORN IN THE YEAR OF THE GOAT

Years of the Goat

1907	1967	2027	2087
1919	1979	2039	2099
1931	1991	2051	
1943	2003	2063	
1955	2015	2075	

(Note: January Capricorns born in any of the above years are natives of the Year of the Horse.)

Elegant and refined, the Asian Goat is known for its creative taste and resourceful mind. Often called the Wayward Artist, the Goat has intellectual brilliance and one-of-a-kind talent. When the aesthetic Chinese Goat is linked to the mountain-climbing Capricorn Goat, the results are remarkable. You have the ability to give reality and substance to your imagination. You combine gentleness and spunk, energy and fantasy. You're a confident explorer as well as a philosopher—you think deeply about things. As a Capricorn Goat, you have theatricality that's not "look-at-me." It's an inventive spirit. Yet a cross you bear is you're rarely satisfied, and this yearning for more (approval, success, affection, magic) is difficult to satisfy. In love, you're a romantic idealist who throws your heart and soul into a relationship. But you tend to choose lovers who are selfish. Compatible partners are born in the Years of the Rabbit, Dragon, Horse, Monkey, and Pig.

IF YOU ARE CAPRICORN BORN IN THE YEAR OF THE MONKEY

Years of the Monkey

1908	1968	2028	2088
1920	1980	2040	2100
1932	1992	2052	
1944	2004	2064	
1956	2016	2076	

(Note: January Capricorns born in any of the above years are natives of the Year of the Goat.)

The Monkey is loved for its vivacity and wit and is considered the most whimsical sign in the Chinese zodiac. Monkey charisma and insouciance mix with your Capricorn steadfastness, making you an unusual combination of spontaneity, playfulness, shrewdness, practicality, and dedication—a strong brew! You're known as an erratic genius, able to excel and become famous, yet also easily sidetracked into whatever new catches your quicksilver attention. You have insatiable curiosity and a remarkable memory, and you are fond of information that impresses people. Indeed, you have a manipulative side and are not above cutting corners with the facts. In love, you're a wild romantic, but it's hard to find happiness. Your interest cools quickly, and only with someone as exciting and intelligent as you can you settle into a committed relationship. Compatible partners are born in the Years of the Rabbit, Dragon, Ox, Pig, Rat, and Tiger.

IF YOU ARE CAPRICORN BORN IN THE YEAR OF THE ROOSTER

Years of the Rooster

1909	1957	2005	2053
1921	1969	2017	2065
1933	1981	2029	2077
1945	1993	2041	2089

(Note: January Capricorns born in any of the above years are natives of the Year of the Monkey.)

Courage is the Rooster's middle name. In Asian mythology, the Rooster rescued the Goddess of the Sun from danger and therefore symbolizes valor. Rooster boldness and mental brilliance join Capricorn aspiration and faith, which makes you expressive, sincere, socially adept, and resilient. Like an unsinkable bathtub toy, you always bounce back up. As a Capricorn Rooster, you're an elegant mixture of the chic and conservative in your style and opinions. And unlike many taciturn Capricorns, you are outspoken, even blunt. Money can cause problems because you're both a spendthrift and a penny-pincher, but your versatile career skills will always bail you out of financial muddles. Love can also be thorny, for you're sensitive and caring but afraid to show it. Then you give too much at the wrong time. With maturity, though, you'll find the lover who makes you feel secure. Compatible partners are born in the Years of the Horse, Ox, and Snake.

Years of the Dog

1910	1958	2006	2054
1922	1970	2018	2066
1934	1982	2030	2078
1946	1994	2042	2090

(Note: January Capricorns born in any of the above years are natives of the Year of the Rooster.)

Like its real-life counterpart, the Asian Dog is faithful, devoted, and utterly reliable. Indeed, Dog loyalty and sense of duty add to your Capricorn commitment, and often your dedication borders on self-sacrifice. You're ambitious, but if someone you care for requires your help, you'll set aside your goals. This may make you feel secretly resentful, but finally your true grit will emerge. As a Capricorn Dog you can be a dynamo, and when inspiration strikes, you pursue it with determination. The sweetest thing about you is your desire to make a lasting contribution to the world. You have a heroic quality and deep ethical values—and those close to you know to ignore your fretful worrying. In love, it takes lots of affection and coddling to make you feel secure. Yet you yourself are an abundant giver who offers total fidelity. Compatible partners are born in the Years of the Cat, Dog, Pig, and Tiger.

Years of the Pig

1911	1959	2007	2055
1923	1971	2019	2067
1935	1983	2031	2079
1947	1995	2043	2091

(Note: January Capricorns born in any of the above years are natives of the Year of the Dog.)

In the West, the pig elicits scorn, but the Asian Pig is the epitome of all that is gallant and good. The Pig is chivalrous, learned, gifted, cultured, and principled. The Pig has huge talent, and Capricorn huge aspirations, and the combination points to a boundless life. This is not to say you don't face struggles, but the sky is the limit. As a Capricorn Pig, you have both genius and persistence. Through early setback (and some insecurity as a child), you learn that by keeping at a task you have the power to excel. You radiate authority, and in your work require mental affinity with associates and plenty of space. In romantic affairs, your style is to trust and give and often overwhelm. You're an extravagant lover, a sexual voluptuary, and passionately committed. This, however, can sometimes border on suffocation. Compatible partners are born in the Years of the Rabbit, Dog, Pig, Ox, and Tiger.

YOU AND NUMEROLOGY

Numerology is the language of numbers. It is the belief that there is a correlation between numbers and living things, ideas, and concepts. Certainly, numbers surround and infuse our lives (e.g., twenty-four hours in a day, twelve months of the year, etc.). And from ancient times, mystics have taught that numbers carry a *vibration*, a deeper meaning that defines how each of us fits into the universe. According to numerology, you are born with a personal number that contains information about who you are and what you need to be happy. This number expresses what numerology calls your life path.

All numbers reduce to one of nine digits, numbers 1 through 9. Your personal number is based on your date of birth. To calculate your number, write your birth date in numerals. As an example, the birth date of December 23, 1983, is written 12-23-1983. Now begin the addition: $12 + 23 + 1 + 9 + 8 + 3 = 56$; 56 reduces to $5 + 6 = 11$; 11 reduces to $1 + 1 = 2$. The personal number for someone born December 23, 1983, is *Two*.

IF YOU ARE A CAPRICORN ONE

Keywords: Confidence and Creativity

One is the number of leadership and new beginnings. You rush into whatever engages your heart and tend to be more impulsive than many Capricorns. You're courageous and inventive, and people respond to your decisiveness if not always to your impatience. You're attracted to unusual pursuits because you like to be one of a kind. You can't bear to be under the thumb of other people's whims and agendas. Careers that call to you are those in which you are in charge and able to work independently. As for love, you want ecstasy and passion, and the most exciting part of a flirtation is the beginning.

IF YOU ARE A CAPRICORN TWO

Keywords: Cooperation and Balance

Two is the number of cooperation and creating a secure entity. Being a Two gives you extra Capricorn magnetism—you attract what you need. Your magic is not only your people skills, but also your ability to breathe life into empty forms (e.g., a concept, an ambitious business idea, a new relationship) and produce something of worth. In your work, you're a perfectionist—and because you have both a creative side *and* a practical side, you're drawn to careers that combine a business sense with an artistic challenge. In love, your deepest desire is for a loving partnership with someone you can trust and share confidences with.

IF YOU ARE A CAPRICORN THREE

Keywords: Expression and Sensitivity

Three symbolizes self-expression. You have a gift for words and a talent for visualization. You link people together so that they benefit from each other. You stimulate others to think. Because you're a connector, you're much loved as a leader, spokesperson, and friend. In a career, Capricorn creativity and innovation are your specialties. You're a quick study, mentally active, and curious about the new. In love, you need someone who excites you intellectually and sensually, and also understands your complex personality. Casual acquaintances may not see your depth, but in love you must have a soulmate who does.

IF YOU ARE A CAPRICORN FOUR

Keywords: Stability and Process

Four is the number of dedication and loyalty. It represents *foundation*, exactly as a four-sided square does. You are a builder, and the direction you go in is up. First you plan, then day by day you add the next step, the next layer, keeping on schedule. You create Capricorn stability by following a process, and your strength is your persistence. Therefore, you're able to control your environment, accomplish great works, and achieve high honor. In love, you look for a relationship with staying power. You need a faithful, giving, and understanding lover with whom you can express your rich sensuality.

IF YOU ARE A CAPRICORN FIVE

Keywords: Freedom and Discipline

Five is the number of change and freedom. With your chameleon intellect (it can go in any direction) and captivating ability to deal with people, you're a marvelous *persuader*. You charm and influence others, and you have great skill with the public. As a Five, you're the Capricorn best able to utilize the ability to initiate. You don't become stuck, and you know how to let go of what doesn't work. In love, you need romantic fantasy but also want a partner who looks ahead to new goals. When you give your heart away, it's to someone with whom you passionately mesh—body and mind.

IF YOU ARE A CAPRICORN SIX

Keywords: Vision and Acceptance

Six is the number of teaching, healing, and utilizing your talents. You're geared toward changing the world, or at least fixing other people's lives. Being an advice giver and even a therapist to your friends comes naturally. You're also competitive, exacting, and demanding—especially with yourself. You're your own harshest critic, for you hold yourself up to a standard of excellence. As a Capricorn *perfector*, you'd like life to run like a well-oiled machine. In love, you're fervent about being a helpmate and confidante, as well as a lover. You're also a secret sensualist who gives your all to someone you trust.

IF YOU ARE A CAPRICORN SEVEN

Keywords: Trust and Openness

Seven is the number of the mystic and the intensely focused specialist. You have an instinct for problem solving, and in a flash understand how things work (in business, between people, etc.). You're an intellectual, a philosopher, and a connoisseur of everything creative. With your Capricorn power of organization, you carve out your own territory. Your work, though, is only part of a deeper search for trust in yourself. At your core, you're extremely loyal and intensely loving, though very selective about relationships. In love, your deepest need is for a partner who can help you on your journey to becoming the real you.

IF YOU ARE A CAPRICORN EIGHT

Keywords: Abundance and Power

Eight is the number of mastery and authority. You are intelligent, alert, quick in action, born to take power in your own hands and guide traffic into the direction you want. You work well in large groups because you see what's needed and can delegate (a major success tool). Others sense you're the one who knows best, and they're right. You think big, tackle the hard stuff, and never let anyone down. As a Capricorn Eight, you're totally true to your word. Giving your promise in love is a very serious act. You are a protective and deeply caring lover, and in turn you need to know your lover is your unwavering ally.

IF YOU ARE A CAPRICORN NINE

Keywords: Integrity and Wisdom

Nine is the path of the "old soul," the number of completion and full bloom. Because it's the last number, it sums up the highs and lows of human experience, and you live a life of dramatic events. You're very intellectual, deeply feeling, extremely protective, interested in all kinds of exploration. People see you as colorful and heroic because you have an adventurous outlook but are also spiritual and altruistic. In love, you're truthful and sincere—and also a romantic, highly sensual creature. As a Capricorn Nine, you generously give of yourself, often to the point of sacrificing.

LAST WORD: YOUR CAPRICORN UNFINISHED BUSINESS

Psychologists often use the phrase *unfinished business* to describe unresolved issues—for example, patterns from childhood that cause unhappiness, anger that keeps one stuck, scenarios of family dysfunction that repeat through second and third generations (such as alcoholism or abusive behavior).

Astrology teaches that the past is indeed very much with us in the present. And that using astrological insights can help us move out of emotional darkness into greater clarity. Even within this book (which is not a tome of hundreds of pages) you have read of many of the superlatives and challenges of being Capricorn. You have breathtaking gifts and at the same time certain tendencies that can undermine utilizing these abilities.

In nature, a fascinating fact is that in jungles and forests a poisonous plant will grow in a certain spot and always, just a few feet away, is a plant that is the antidote to that specific poison. Likewise, in astrology, the antidote is right there ready to be used when the negatives threaten to overwhelm your life.

Capricorn's unfinished business has to do with your *drive*—the enviable locomotive force with which you press forward. Your indefatigable energy infuses everything you do, and your indomitable will can wear down whatever opposes you. It's in your Capricorn DNA to keep climbing to the top, to reach your goal, to get the gain. If everyone could emulate your enterprising habits, the human race would be twice as productive.

Yet Capricorn has a hunger difficult to satiate. Even when you've achieved an ambition, generally you're not satisfied. It's not enough. You arrive at the top only to discover another mountain to be conquered, and so you continue to the next and the next. In a way, the rewards become secondary to accomplishing the continual *next* thing, and your life is marked by a discontented kind of striving.

You can be a merciless taskmaster—on yourself and others. In this mode, you are exacting, gruff, unfair, and stingy. You're likely envious of what others have that you don't. Inside, you're tense and high-strung.

Because Capricorn is security oriented and bent on accomplishing, it's intrinsic to your nature to be materialistic. You look on the trappings of prosperity as the most desirable things to have. You tend to see people in terms of their image (are they rich and successful?). You can become a clever opportunist who cultivates the right people. Even romantically, especially early in life, you're attracted to those who seem glamorous and powerful and make you look good.

Your own image is terribly important. You're seriously concerned with the face you show to the world and work hard at your upward mobility; you do your utmost to present yourself as someone superior and superlative. For you to feel demeaned by anyone is devastating, and it can take years to recover.

Adding to the complicated emotional stew is your conflicted struggle with self-esteem—both the lack and the hubris. You're vulnerable and insecure as well as having overweening pride. It isn't easy for you to develop close relationships; you fear rejection and can be distrustful. Nor do you talk much about feelings. The sharing of private information is monumentally difficult, and instead of reaching out you withdraw. Frequently, you suffer from isolation.

You shove down dark and fearful feelings—often you don't acknowledge you're even feeling them. You escape through work, new projects, busyness. You keep finding something to begin—or to finish. But at times, despite your efforts, your melancholic and depressive moods take over.

Yet the antidotes are there to be found in their entirety in being Capricorn, for you are the sign of *commitment*—to work, love, idealistic values, and making your life count for something. When you're on a quest, you can change the world. You may not realize how intensely loving your heart is, but when you begin to feel safe and you open it little by little, you are tender and giving. Whether to a project or a person, you offer deep loyalty and endless support. Your promises are for keeps.

You inspire others to realize the power of discipline. In you, they see in action that dedicated work will make dreams come true.

People respond to your special brand of wit and wisdom, leadership and great panache. You're at home in the world of tangibles. You see the larger, long-term picture, are a realist, and can deal with *what is*. When others need a rational head in a crisis, they call on you. At your best, you match your heroic words with heroic actions. Among your greatest strengths are your decency and moral courage.

In friendships and relationships, you're the one on whom people depend. You do not betray confidences or speak disparagingly about others behind their backs. You are made of better stuff.

Blessed with a richly inquiring spirit, you are wise and insightful. When your heart is open and your mind is disciplined, you are capable of achieving everything you need to be happy. Capricorn of noble heritage, you were born in the dead of winter, and deep within, you life is ready to burst into bloom.

FAMOUS PEOPLE WITH THE SUN IN CAPRICORN

Muhammad Ali
Steve Allen
Matthew Arnold
Isaac Asimov
Joan Baez
Simone de Beauvoir
Robert Bly
Humphrey Bogart
Ray Bolger
Victor Borge
David Bowie
Tycho Brahe
Louis Braille
Lloyd Bridges
Nicolas Cage
Al Capone
Jim Carrey
Carlos Castaneda
Paul Cezanne
Anton Chekhov
Mary Higgins Clark
Kevin Costner
Katie Couric
Ted Danson
Ellen DeGeneres
John Denver
Marlene Dietrich
Faye Dunaway
Robert Duvall
Benjamin Franklin
Diane von Furstenberg
Ava Gardner
Kahlil Gibran
Barry Goldwater

Cary Grant
Oliver Hardy
Stephen Hawking
Conrad Hilton
J. Edgar Hoover
Anthony Hopkins
Howard Hughes
Joan of Arc
Janis Joplin
Danny Kaye
Diane Keaton
Johann Kepler
Val Kilmer
Martin Luther King Jr.
Rudyard Kipling
Gelsey Kirkland
Andre Kostelanetz
Gene Krupa
Frank Langella
Matt Lauer
Jude Law
Gypsy Rose Lee
Robert E. Lee
John Legend
Oscar Levant
Shari Lewis
Jack London
Howie Long
Mao Tse-tung
Ricky Martin
Henri Matisse
Dave Matthews
Henry Miller
A. A. Milne

Moliere
Mary Tyler Moore
Kate Moss
Sir Isaac Newton
Richard M. Nixon
Aristotle Onassis
Dolly Parton
Louis Pasteur
Edgar Allan Poe
Elvis Presley
Jean-Pierre Rampal
Paul Revere
Helena Rubinstein
Anwar Sadat
Carl Sandburg
Dianne Sawyer
Albert Schweitzer
Rod Serling
J. D. Salinger
Al Smith
Maggie Smith
Sissy Spacek
Joseph Stalin
Rod Stewart
Alfred Stieglitz
Michael Stipe
J. R. R. Tolkien
Jon Voight
Denzel Washington
Woodrow Wilson
Tiger Woods
Loretta Young

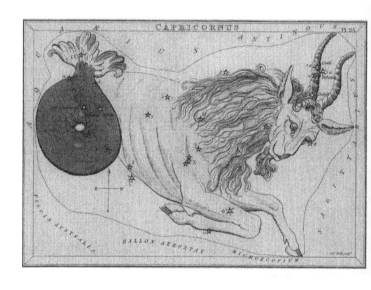

PART TWO

ALL ABOUT YOUR SIGN
OF CAPRICORN

CAPRICORN'S ASTROLOGICAL AFFINITIES, LINKS, AND LORE

SYMBOL: The Goat (in Ancient Times, the Sea-Goat) 🐐

A strong, surefooted animal able to butt its way through obstructions and ascend the heights by taking advantage of every foothold. The older symbol, the mythological Sea-Goat, represents dual forces in Capricorn: the grounded, practical person who aspires to the heights, and the creative, intuitive being who can swim in the waters of emotion.

RULING PLANET: Saturn ♄

The Roman god who presided over the sowing and reaping of grain. In ancient times, Saturn was the outermost planet of the known universe—and the god was linked to the concept of Father Time. Our modern depiction at New Year's of an aged man representing the departing year has roots in the figure of Saturn. An old belief is that time ended with Capricorn, an idea fostered by the fact that Saturn (Capricorn's ruler) was the final planet of the ancient zodiac and was also the god of time. In astrology, Saturn represents discipline, responsibility, patience, industry, obstacles, limitation, and restriction.

DOMINANT KEYWORD

I USE

GLYPH (Written Symbol) ♑

The pictograph represents the V-shaped beard of the Goat and the curved tail of the Sea-Goat. As well, the glyph pictures the sun slowly rising upward from the depths—a symbol of the winter solstice, the day Capricorn begins. The glyph is also a representation of the human knee and circular kneecap (the part of the anatomy that Capricorn rules). In symbolic terms, the glyph is two straight lines that meet one another, connected to a circle and a crescent. This represents the melding of authority and responsibility that is strengthened by both energy and passion.

PART OF THE BODY RULED BY CAPRICORN: The Bones, Joints, and Knees

Capricorn natives often have beautiful bone structure but are subject to stiff joints, rheumatism, and orthopedic problems.

LUCKY DAY: Saturday

The day named for Saturn, ruler of Capricorn.

LUCKY NUMBERS: 2 AND 8

Numerologically, 2 is the number of wisdom, leadership, achievement, and balance—and 8 is the number of strength, confidence, authority, and mastery. These qualities align with the nature of Capricorn.

TAROT CARD: The World

The card in the Tarot linked to Capricorn is the World. Ancient names for this card are the Great One of the Night of Time and Crown of the Magi. In the Tarot, this card signifies the discovery of one's purpose in life. It speaks of having knowledge of what you want and the courage to do it. The World points to the goal reached at the end of a struggle. When this card turns up in a Tarot reading, it symbolizes the start of a new experience and triumph in the undertaking.

The card itself pictures a dancing maiden clad in a scarf and surrounded by a wreath of leaves. In each hand she holds a magic wand, and in the four corners are the figures of the four Fixed signs in astrology. The dancer represents final attainment, the wreath victory, and the wands the balance between the material and the spiritual. The four figures are witnesses to the realization of the dream.

For Capricorn, the World tells you that when you've learned life's lessons and your mind and heart are in balance, the path of liberation opens and you will find what fulfills you.

MAGICAL BIRTHSTONE: Garnet

The garnet is a gemstone prized for its unique dark-red color and its use as a talisman. Although garnets come in other colors, the red garnet is best known. The word *garnet* comes from *pomegranate*, a fruit that the gemstone resembles. The garnet has extremely high refractivity that reflects a great amount of light—therefore, the gem is thought to provide light in the darkness and be protective. From ancient times, the red garnet has symbolized the life-bringing qualities of blood, and it was used as a healing stone to stimulate blood circulation and the heart. Thus the garnet is linked to the arousal of passion. For Capricorns, the garnet is said to attract popularity, high esteem, and true love.

SPECIAL COLORS: Dark Green and Brown

Classic, comforting colors of nature and the earth. Dark green symbolizes growth and fertility, and brown practicality.

CONSTELLATION OF CAPRICORN

Capricornus is the Latin word for "horned goat," and from Babylonian times this constellation has been a Sea-Goat. The Sea-Goat was associated with the Babylonian god Ea, who brought culture out of the sea to humankind. (The constellation of Aquarius is also linked to Ea.) The Greek myth of the Sea-Goat is that Pan, the goat-god, was attacked by the sea-monster Typhon. Pan dove into the water, and the parts of him above the water remained a goat and those under the water were transformed into a fish. This story has its roots in the joining together of Babylon, situated on the river Euphrates, and Nineveh, situated on the river Tigris, under one sovereignty. The Sea-Goat symbolizes the melding in Capricorn of earth (practical matters) with water (emotional matters).

CITIES

Oxford, Mexico City, Boston, Brussels, Chicago

COUNTRIES

Mexico, India, Afghanistan, Bulgaria

FLOWERS

Carnation, Ivy, and Heartsease

TREES

Pine, Elm, and Poplar

HERBS AND SPICES

Comfrey and Hemp

METAL: Lead

An extremely weighty, stable metal (often called a base metal) that from earliest civilization has been used in construction, weaponry, pipes, and plumbing and as ballast, building blocks, and weights. Lead's properties of being relatively simple to extract, resistant to corrosion, dense yet highly malleable, and easy to work with have made it tremendously useful for thousands of years. Its use dates back to at least 6400 B.C. Alchemists, who linked lead to Saturn, considered it the world's oldest metal and tried (unsuccessfully) to turn it into gold. Lead is everlasting—science says it can outlive the life of the universe—a feature in keeping with the quality of Capricorn.

ANIMALS RULED BY CAPRICORN

Goats and animals with cloven hoofs

DANGER

Others may harbor hidden grudges and resentments because of Capricorn's coldness and reserve. Secrets from the past are often used against Capricorns.

PERSONAL PROVERBS

Intelligence without ambition is a bird without wings.

Ability will get you to the top, but only endurance will keep you there.

KEYWORDS FOR CAPRICORN

Purposeful
Ambitious
Sense of responsibility
Determined
Hardworking
Dedicated
Analytical
Motivated
Long-term winner
Organized
Able to govern
Attracted to structure
Long memory
Moralistic
Self-sufficient
Practical
Realistic
Shrewd
Domineering
Authoritative

Materialistic
Rigid
Frugal
Controlling
Critical
Conformist
Contradictory
Vulnerable
Humorous
Sarcastic
Moody
Depressive

HOW ASTROLOGY SLICES AND DICES YOUR SIGN OF CAPRICORN

DUALITY: Feminine

The twelve astrological signs are divided into two groups, *masculine* and *feminine*. Six are masculine and six are feminine; this is known as the sign's *duality*. A masculine sign is direct and energetic. A feminine sign is receptive and magnetic. These attributes were given to the signs about 2,500 years ago. Today, modern astrologers avoid the sexism implicit in these distinctions. A masculine sign does not mean "positive and forceful" any more than a feminine sign means "negative and weak." In modern terminology, the masculine signs are defined as outer-directed and strong through action. The feminine signs, such as your sign of Capricorn, are self-contained and strong through inner reserves.

TRIPLICITY (ELEMENT): Earth

The twelve signs are also divided into groups of three signs each. These three-sign groups are called a *triplicity*, and each of these denotes an *element*. The elements are *Fire*, *Earth*, *Air*, and *Water*. In astrology, an element symbolizes a fundamental characterization of the sign.

The three *Fire* signs are Aries, Leo, and Sagittarius. Fire signs are active and enthusiastic.

The three *Earth* signs are Taurus, Virgo, and Capricorn. Earth signs are practical and stable.

The three *Air* signs are Gemini, Libra, and Aquarius. Air signs are intellectual and communicative.

The three *Water* signs are Cancer, Scorpio, and Pisces. Water signs are emotional and intuitive.

....

QUADRUPLICITY (QUALITY): Cardinal

....

The twelve signs are also divided into groups of four signs each. These four-sign groups are called a *quadruplicity*, and each of these denotes a *quality*. The qualities are *Cardinal*, *Fixed*, and *Mutable*. In astrology, the quality signifies the sign's interaction with the outside world.

Four signs are *Cardinal** signs. They are Aries, Cancer, Libra, and Capricorn. Cardinal signs are enterprising and outgoing. They are the initiators and leaders.

Four signs are *Fixed*. They are Taurus, Leo, Scorpio, and Aquarius. Fixed signs are resistant to change. They hold on; they are perfectors and finishers rather than originators.

Four signs are *Mutable*. They are Gemini, Virgo, Sagittarius, and Pisces. Mutable signs are flexible, versatile, and adaptable. They are able to adjust to differing circumstances.

*When the Sun crosses the four cardinal points in the zodiac, we mark the beginning of each of our four seasons. Aries begins spring; Cancer begins summer; Libra begins fall; Capricorn begins winter.

Your sign of Capricorn is a Feminine, Earth, Cardinal sign—and no other sign in the zodiac is this exact combination. Your sign is a one-of-a-kind combination, and therefore you express the characteristics of your duality, element, and quality differently from any other sign.

For example, your sign is a *Feminine* sign, meaning you are resourceful, resilient, protective. You're an *Earth* sign, meaning you're responsible, practical, and stable. And you're a *Cardinal* sign, meaning you're energetic and enterprising, a mover and shaker and activist who will initiate.

Now the sign of Taurus is also Feminine and Earth, but unlike Capricorn (which is Cardinal), Taurus is Fixed. Like you, Taurus is loyal, devoted, and creative, and especially focused on building a secure life—but Taurus has a stubborn, immovable nature. Taurus is the sign of being rooted and staying with what's familiar. Its motivation is to avoid risk and preserve what has been tested by time. It easily becomes opinionated, inflexible, and habit bound. Taurus doesn't have your willingness to seize an idea and instigate an action. You, being Cardinal, have an appetite for innovation, though not because of its "newness." Indeed, you're fond of tradition and distrust far-out ideas, but you are willing to take a chance on something that might add to the glory of your achievement. Your motivation is to make things happen, to be recognized and remembered.

Virgo, too, is Feminine and Earth, but unlike Capricorn (which is Cardinal), Virgo is Mutable. Like you, Virgo is diligent and thorough, has an incisive mind and a practical approach, and puts great commitment into work. However, being Mutable, Virgo has a tendency to scatter its energy; it can be sidetracked (especially by its fussy perfectionism) and lose sight of the big picture. Virgo doesn't have your drive and self-assertion. You, on the other hand, are Cardinal and refuse to get stuck in a dead-end situation. With your fierce ambition, you ignore barriers and propel toward your long-term goals. You have the ability to start things in a dynamic way and then turn your ideas into a reality out in the real world.

POLARITY: Cancer

The twelve signs are also divided into groups of two signs each. These two-sign groups are called a *polarity* (meaning "opposite"). Each sign in the zodiac has a polarity, which is its opposite sign in the other half of the zodiac. The two signs express opposite characteristics.

Capricorn and Cancer are a polarity. Capricorn is the sign of strength, authority, duty, and ambition. The themes of being action-oriented and restless, having impressive power, and being able to organize and take command run through your personality. You're the sign that governs reputation, career, standing in the community. Capricorn is the one who bears responsibility and has the persistence to achieve goals. Curiously, you're a rebel *and* an establishment person. The rebel part is your determination to be in the forefront and forge your own way—you don't take orders; you *give* orders. The establishment part is your belief in tradition, law and order, standards, and structure.

As a Capricorn, you seek honor, praise, and approval in the world at large—it's in the emotional world that you tend to be reserved. You hold back your feelings and exercise control; in general, you don't allow emotion to flow spontaneously. You derive security of self from your work and accomplishments, from being valued for your achievements and needed for the guidance you give to others.

Cancer, your opposite sign, is the sign of the home—of family life, domesticity, childhood—as well as the process of giving birth (to ideas, creative projects, and offspring). Cancer rules instinct, emotions, intuition, dreams, and expressiveness. Cancerians rarely use direct force; their nature is to avoid confrontation and get to their goal by moving sideways. They dwell in the realm of the imagination and possess deep understanding of the human heart. Among this sign's best qualities is a "mothering" instinct, the nurturing and protectiveness it provides to those they love. Cancer finds security in the love and closeness of mates, family members, and intimate friends.

Astrologically, you as a Capricorn can benefit from adopting some of Cancer's comfort with feelings. Cancer easily senses others' thoughts and desires. It can be *simpatico*—Cancer feels what another person is feeling. By following Cancer's example of listening to intuition and insight, you'll pick up emotional subtleties that otherwise elude a Capricorn. In relationships, Cancer's warm affection and trust engender devoted caring from others. In contrast, Capricorn tends to set controls and boundaries in alliances (a lover or friend must live up to your perfectionist standards). You can become dictatorial, which is apt to result in what you least want: rejection. Being more Cancer-like in your relationships will bring you more emotional security.

Another worthy feature of Cancer to adopt is its freedom of expression creatively. Cancer happily gives rein to its imagination and vision, inspiring others through art, music, writing. Both Capricorn and Cancer are ambitious, though you're fiercer in your pursuit and more concerned with your public image and the financial aspects. But you do your own deep creativity a disservice when you put money ahead of the artistry. Like you, Cancer is very fond of money, yet usually discovers that when creativity comes first, money follows. This is a lesson for you to take to heart, for too often the equation doesn't work the other way around.

In turn, Cancer has much to learn from you, and at the top of this list is handling fear. You rely on your discipline to keep you going not only in the face of obstacles but in battling inner terrors. Thus, you derive confidence from the very fact that you don't stop in your tracks. You know that action dissolves anxiety, and you always take action. Like Cancer, you're tenacious, but your tenacity is an *involvement* of yourself in the problem, an instinct to fix what is wrong, whereas Cancer tends to hang on because it's afraid to let go. Capricorn doesn't get lost in unworkable theories and hopeless attachments the way Cancer might. Your basic motivation is to do the right thing—and prove to the world that determination and discipline will always take you to the place you dream of.